Otherwise In 2

David Appelbaum

ISBN: 978-81-8253-948-8

First Edition: 2022
Rs. 200/-

Cyberwit.net
HIG 45 Kaushambi Kunj, Kalindipuram
Allahabad - 211011 (U.P.) India
http://www.cyberwit.net
Tel: +(91) 9415091004
E-mail: info@cyberwit.net

Printed at Thomson Press India Limited.

Contents

I. Separate Entrances

a want (illusory)

a glob of fig jam dropt

a hundred ants or a
veritable coven

swirls elliptically
dense with pinching spells

a feeding frenzy
an archaic wish to clothe

Eve's pudendum

as fig must signify

with their brittle bodies

in the garden eternal

it lives in my clumsiness
with fruits
(desires for all species)

to pluck and to taste
one by one

what comes to be called
pleasure

(to some, sin)

it's all about the father

a colorless cocoon
straddling the underside
of an oak leaf

the sexless euphony
of moths

who enter the abyss
without parricide

we are different

simple hatred
where no one is to blame
throws the die

their one flesh
erases a boundary

it is there for us

we are the mortal ones
separate by day

a single pronoun
economy hours bed

there, a wet stain
an inland sea

seems the only thing
in the room

and millennia
try to efface it

purity

texts not used

dispossessed
in a lost and found

wanting an owner
to meet
at the landfill

someone to pout on
a pinky ring
and say *it's mine*

it fell off the shelf

the gem I'm looking for

perfect to set
in an ode or sonnet

. . . .

if meaning is
a sensed relation

it isn't a heartbreak

to be repurposed
pulpwood

swished in a chemical
wash
for another day

to breed
like the young and beautiful

each shred admiring
its own ghost

whispering falsetto
no no no no
until the word means

anything at all

an auto-reset,
stupid

the shortest distance

between two
is rejection

a self lags behind
itself
swaddled in shame

it's natural

jonquils stunned
by frost, drooping heads

the broken wing
tossed from the nest

. . . .

if there and here
were the same
we all would be winners

the loser's revenge
a non-story

the hero's destiny
a commonplace

getting would have
no *how*

but be part of
the wallpaper

a journey without
surprise

life would take forever
while dying
of boredom

that each drop

in the ocean

is what makes up
the ocean

a long movie

. . . .

the round shiny
stones
in the mason jar

I covered with
sea water

so they could drink

the saucer on top
is to keep them
feeling wet

. . . .

I want to suck
each pebble

until it's dry
as air

to figure how
the earth began

I'm fading

like a sing-along

opening to show
a pair of
stubby yellow wings

it's beautiful
when one thing
changes

into another

leaving you
ready
to fly off

under a new
name

or the same
revised by tired
ears

that no longer
say
right, I heard

but wait,
wasn't it I
who called?

top dog

under a bench
a small white dog digs

'desire is doubled in love'

not to middle earth
but to lie in

and done, now brown
(reward of honest labor)

when a big dog barks him out
'love is doubled in anger'

but not fitting the hole
cedes it back
for further excavation

reunited with the sentiment
more dirt flies
capriciously

to further sully
poor relation

yet both desires persist
in each mind

even after desire has or doesn't

been satisfied

in the underworld

Cerberus waits
droolingly

the extra dot

on naïve

is hilarious
(I don't mean
to be critical)

why is there
something
rather than nothing

or for that matter
anything at all?

if you double-
cross a 't'
it's a religions

icon
millions pray to

so I suppose
with the 'i'

wide-eyed wonder
is in charge

like a child
with a buttercup

the loving look
reaches through

both those dark
tunnels

gateways to the
soul

glow worm

each salty roadside moment
says *I'm desperate*

I'm treasure

in broad daylight
nothing shows

chicory buckwheat
scarlet pimpernel
share what's hiding

with spring clarity
to perfect the mind

come later, at nightfall
your blurred peripheral
vision

the uneasy stars
see counterparts below

that blink slowly
as you kneel over their

green-yellow light
'being single'

it ceases to glow
gives no name to say

the one thing
you never can know

the eye on a beeline

for its object

nerves see
because love is a stain

wait
do bees fly in a line
on a line

an airline, a timeline
a sight line?

keep a vigil
on your back
on the lawn as they pass over

watch for dives
detours back flips
loop-dee-doops
solo takedowns

evasive action

is the shortest distance
between the points

you've tried to draw
a line, really

a thin red one

where do these words come from
anyway?

'mouths of babes'

who speak without real lines

but babble
crookedly

slither is one of those words

you mix slime with
whither

but the little garter snake
would have nothing of that

being accord and grace
draped
expertly
over the tarmac crack

seeming like *it*

a neutral thing
slung like a jay
flattened by its weight

a stop-action shot

where you see motion
at its purest

as the mind recoils
into a future imaginary

a pick-up in a scene
when stills cease

to exceed any origin

and become the rod
Moses held in his hand

before God made it
a random thing

slithering
snake-like
serpentine

hummingbird to the window

I'm all used up

hearing me say *I'm done*

meaning dry finished history

flown in from South America
distance and time
vibrate with true feeling

my own thoughts
and fingerprints
their glorious stuff

we look
(if bird eyes are frontal)
and nod words across
the thin glass pane

—can we come down
from the clouds now?

—yes, but only for a short
visit

celebration of false wealth

like a weather-related event
is all in good fun

a crowing of April
after heavy winter swells

no need to cool your heels
on earth, but serenade

the angels know your net worth

it's irony that truth
is beauty and not its opposite

Keats hit on a metaphor
and it responded seductively

what if one loves what one thinks

a list of worth, assets
like blue glittery fruit, proof

besides, no one today can count

everyone uses a calculator

a line

libation cups
papier-mâché
on a strip of
corrugated cardboard

twelve gods
prepare to drink
to the dog
in hell

song alone calms

song alone says
mercy

dolor and bliss
reunited
sisters of one womb

his bark is powder
the halls bring
a steady reign of it

his food grows
between the two

he eats nothing
thinning thinking

a hollow below
his neck

the same as the dog
in heaven
who eats anything

bland milquetoast
no butter

lesson

one small crow
to a larger one
listening

isn't it time
(that doesn't exist)

to learn
once and for all

the difference
it makes

to pass over
the seed bed
for the corn silk
and kernels

to survey it all?

whereas the other
heard

to crow
is to count

the future present
among one's possessions

and eat here now

let's

II. Stalled Events

pop into your mouth

'pop' speaks rich
sounds

lineage, violence, sweets . . .
crunch a dry crust

a balloon
going out

a question
melting the air

release sudden
irreversible:
the plot

a man and a woman
finish wine
get up

he says, I'd follow
you anywhere

her breath
fills a cavity
that was empty

bundles of spiders

snake

along the roof
of my mouth

try to find
another verb

for what description
can't do

strip the mind
of its pinwheels

be barer
of poor things

like a thick tongue

I'll never look the same
at a tree

without seeing
Louise Bourgeois'

the world

continually created

cat's cradle

strings vibrate
constants impose

visitors report
communal
ventures

bows, weaves
purls and knits
aces
knots

even the lovers'

which unties
attachment

each
teaches alone

God
is the spacing

what matter is there?

—light
festive as a doll

primo

apotheosis
forgets

dust motes
float
like scattered ore
of thought

emotion is opposite
cutting life
chisel
on cold stone

chips fly
off the shoulder

the mass the block
the torso

three birds

make intense roadside ritual

a *mikvah*
or animal sacrifice
call the *simurgh*?

what do I know
about birds?

they fly
they sing
they hop

dust rises
as with a conflagration

light
(from their angle)
is eclipsed

from the whirlwind
perhaps
God speaks
crow

dreams of flight
are born
and jeered at

migration debated
nesting debunked

yeah, three birds
their point of view
(more likely)

dirt
young sun
fleas

all itch

right at the rotary

sometimes I don't know
the things on
my mind

they merge
in orderly fashion

if none is more
pushy than the rest

the circle isn't perfect
nor the signage

how five lines
of thinking
circumnavigate

miraculous
without a fight

. . .

on a Riemannian
surface
nothing is parallel

neither love nor
hate
remain apart

all roads
lead elsewhere

to think is
to lose the knack

of coalescence

concentrate

. . .

claim to priority
stop
look left

test brakes

acquiesce

surrender

heliotrope

who am I
to follow
the old sun

down his bunker
the tomb

where *yes*
changes to *no*?

desert birds
circle
dim thought

the beast
that is night
slouches darkly

an idea
that never sees
form

water petals
drop

forward step
grey sky
power lines
cross

will itself
unmoved

how to get
there

assesses
what to leave
behind

if you count
backwards

the lesser gray light

reflective
on a vase:

a take on
the Greek fragment
lauding Phaeton

his exploit
the sun's horses
wild rant

calm minds
have no place
in history

as image
his face makes
noise

like grapes
getting drunk

how I'd seal
a beam
in a jar

the next sunbath
at the shore

just to drink
him in

a love lost
at Pompey

go do it

versed in same

who am I
to make paper
from bulrush?

presto
a basket appears
then the queen
of Egypt

three glossy laced-up
ones, slanted
on top
make good harness

Moishe,
who'll stop
the pigs

from blowing it
down?

so much pulp
for copy

is this covenant
to be written
in stone?

is it rain

in which we dissolve
like a bad witch?

storms they say
project martial pleasure

what can words do?

evidence converges on
a mortar line
whose proof
a chimney
leak

yet many humans
embrace
secret plots
to drive out
news of inhumanity

chinks
in the window
metaphor
ease the low
pressure

this life
mizzles

the bicycle man

pumps
the universe
made of strings
plucked
like an Irish harp

not certain
of a voice: *om*
he splices
two streets together
for a high
C

mi

dark matter
fills his lungs

black hole-gullet

errancy
is in his delivery
pouch

mine?

light contracts
red torus to
green

his is this event
the next
epoch
twitters

the same
note

flat

umm

[mother—Arabic]
I am at sea again

help me
eau-mère

a refugee
crossing
life's waters

dying
to express this

. . .

need and love
made the earth
its oceans
for a start

rictus split
leaving one
barefoot, pregnant

womb
some think we
return
in peace

speaking
one thing needful

. . .

strife
is a sound
absent in humming

when thought
is mum
discourse dead
self-resorbed

yet escape
to the unknown
requires
authority

someone
to practice

the fricative
other

cocoon

III. Point Oblique

what is your most intelligent thought?

leave it a moment

there in the jet stream
whining through the air

wash a smudge from your face—
does one avoid redaction?

glossy cobalt-blue globe
reflects
the word pool

spawning new brain cells
drenched in things
and avowals

a Babel thrusts
the bales away

passcodes shriek of God

or some grand personage
Charlemagne or Attila the Hun

the emperor shall speak
and it is expectant
as a naked dial tone

when speech
wise with the voice
of betrayal

leaves cortical scars

a splashy border

essence made plastic
at the local drugstore

groans and cries
tin trumpets boom
the game's decision

a player (sad? happy?)
drops a scrap of paper
between us

in Farsi it says
'dream'

in the dream it says
'erode'
the line

get up and go

'where'?

a non-descript region
this space called the heart

pathos is iffy

compass berserk
in the magnetic storm

how far you will get
(kitchen unhinged)

depends
on long azalea-lined aisles

promises to escape
an image

of fustian caves
that extrudes impulse

no answer

just wait

you will arrive at never
with only this poem

awake in your dream

the back door opens

in

the present is cupped
to exclude you
outside parenthesis

tongues click
on roofs of mouth

as you give alms

there are many
failing poor

as you give solace
how far will you
feel no exit plan

from the thought
of armor

how far will you hear
cries within

brackets walled
to keep a palm
being outstretched?

the dark before dawn

turns specular

squirrels rat race
astride a tree trunk
no backwash
from the sentence

o yes, evil is there
a zilch
when the run stands still

like a blind stain

but the leaf-scape
is true to that

fully delineated
colors of
Jacob's coat

old grapes
loose in their skin

a must affirms
obscurity

an oculus stares at
the journal entry

a man and a woman
hold hands together

a slender chain
of syllables
their pledge

empty liveries

sound loudest

like pink shirts
on bald men

such beauty
in anomaly

strung raindrops
on a phone wire

from deep time
will prevail

a birth-name
can't be unsaid

once whispered
in the infant's ear

once heard
on the grapevine

tympanum
truth

black in the middle

a floret
like wild carrot

it is cure to bedlam's
dank tunnel
into the mind void

'wither' strums
staticky as a cough

'as' as in archer
hard by the heel

yet 'it's' empty
after fledglings fly

suns gather no more
to fill
the blind spot

left so the universe
can't look

back at me
when I blink

as it goes on a spree
with the mad lady

moon boots and all

summer freak

hides in the woodbine

basting
a heart now and then

a wind at systole
banal as Beckett

a scream at diastole

you'll step ahead
onto the crumbling earth
times inertia

a-crawl
maladroit

a post-season pennant
waves in your hand

resistant to
your uncertain outline

sense so evanescent
love must be

just saying
what it says when alone

without your ear
to the keyhole

drinking in the blood

tree tops slither across

the sky
a path you carved there

by faith alone we live
in the fine dust
that falls clingingly

evoked by names
of fauna
on ancient lists

spurred in hope

tangled clouds notched
along the corridor
to the heart

next tome you pick
from the basement
bring a book on snakes

the small iris

budded abruptly

hey, the middle-
of-winter sale

'everything must go'

sky scrapes off
the underpile
of leaves

roof like a knife
dulled and gray

time is no
solution

but a web
to hold each
precious nub

a tendency
to take exception

a wild hair
down your chin
to your chest

IV. Palaver

'lost earring

on the fifth floor'

such comings and goings
show beauty's risky path

it has no backing:
a design flaw

stop, think a moment
the pierced lobe
takes in all that is said

moans, mutterings
curse words, prayers
sighs, guttural stops

a collector of phrases
passwords
shibboleths

ask what slipped off
into the reflecting pool

where lovers go
with coins

hear
what the ear knows

the beloved
awaits you found

in *dreck*
of the sub-basement

come

birdbath revisited

dust to dust

do they do
a before and after

floured and basted
with King Arthur's

or just fly off
a plume
on a moon shot

caring only to be seen?

champions of earth
occupied with

a persistent desire
for stratospheric
purity

clean is close
to preen

a skinny dip
in dead humus

it's beautiful
to remain in character

rather than bang
your head

against a shaggy tree.
to see stars

meant only for a hero
come Valhalla

in a nutshell

picked clean
halved crania
roil the carpeted lawn

louche
a one-eyed look
at the dictionary

jack o'spades

there, all things
printed in serif

are demons' discourse
on forbidden themes

'pleasure'
'focus'
'triumph'

what happens to
family values

e.g., green grass
white picket fence?

as if laissez-faire
were cause
of debris

or the hickory tree
itself

or gravity
making due
with fell things

'pea brain'

that small voice
behind the ear

focus on
the inhuman clarity
of cracks in the road

my throat grows hoarse
in sublimity

. . .

love the theme song
like citrus
fresh, clean aura

there is no shame
in assault

just don't believe
the echo

'that little nothing'
creeps

like a mirage
it's air pressure

. . .

another angle:
'the pea-green sea'

symbolism
and paranoia
as sisters

(in denial)

follow your madness
if you want a cross

moon shot

(luna chat)

reaching over myself
for the hidden face

tracked by Chinese
search vehicles

there are only glyphs
tigers and dingbats

lobed shadows of self

serial numbers
video cams embedded

why would anyone go
to the moon?

there's no sky
air water
truth

it turns lover
into geometry
the perfect disk

in this life

the sun alone rises
to lift a skirt

the moon I see
has only ill-humor

gone rogue

(craning to read)

my seatmate's note:

'shame falters . . .
admission comes late'

gaze down the steps
down the stops, deepenings
down the grooves on the roof

edges of mirrors
that deprecate the view

check to see
check to see
the birds say

a single Judas kiss
both sets of lips are mine

I like to think
exempt

means 'let'

whether enough time
has passed

. . .

full title:
the devil lives
in other people's mail

sleeves of fire
wait there

at least the smolder
of dead beliefs

sighing
to be heard

under my skin

like an awning
coffee *al fresco*

a tinder membrane
ready to burn

a grain of sand
obsessing a pearl

which?

reclining lessens
pressure

I suppose blood
slows the brain's
pained furrows

teetering on the thin red line

above pockets
of self-reference

how far will you get
before _______?

what is skin anyway

a sieve

a few microns
of aging epidermis

plus special feeling cells
for thorns, etc.

telling what
you may be, or not

the tortured flirtation

as if it could be done
without

jump on the pile

don’t stop acting
from envy

when did you learn
the trace
was yours

just as
the colors and sounds?

when did you forget?

. . .

why desire returns
after harm:

any inertial
system tends
toward self-
destruction

move off dead
center

when the dial
says ‘persist’

. . .

the pleasure
hiding in new
names for things

feeling distance
an ally

you can see
without touching

without being
alive

a lot of hype

sounds like 'hope'
but isn't

how much
depends on number
theory

or surveying

if you collect
bunches
whatevers

the form is
inspirited

warning:
proceed counting

with hunched shoulders
(the cynic)

who dogs you

Diogenes had
a lantern
worth a thousand words

his fate
was to slim
truth to the size
of a shadow

the perpetrator
had to stand
out of the light

of a public nuisance

where is his
magic lamp now?

'the deepest is the skin'

wise paintings

bury crystals
to prism from within
a slanting field of snow

side by side
a conifer's
branching pipettes

need: a retort

surface surrounds
itself
a Moebius strip

who else tries
to get within

when there's no volume
to that?

like holes
in the biosphere

nothing inside
but rays
that pour down

nothing to prevent you
rubbing on sunscreen

sugar lift coy smile

and countless small white
bulbs go off

intersection
invites narrative

you're chained to the mast
ears unstopped

pen in hand

slugs and palettes
uploaded

what she meant
to convince you
we're each alone

(taken with a grain
of salt)

is a poetic
liaison

scrawled on the helm
for you to believe

the impossible
possible

a rebus

when things
emerge
into cold light

this lethal drift
when rocks clap

behind
the ghost on high

and leave you deaf

when the long way

is short
due to bottlenecks

held up on the cervix
while being born

you come out
short on breath
upside down

tilting gravity
like a leviathan

the rest, to exhale
slowly
reel to the right

to count that present
among
one's trial

to flip
the tiddledee winks
and land flat

to cry
the one thing
we don't know

combing the beach
for shells

the stars are infinite
calcite

bloodnoun

one dark night
for dedicated
content

I walked
by the cattails
the frogs made home

my breath
their bullhorn

the moon came out

a metaphor
darting
to the noösphere

acoustically poor

another time
it was content
made form

the breath
coming to rest
underwater

stentorian bleeps

like automated
distress calls

hacked my thoughts

slivered moon

a selfie

shared my shame
with God

heartstrings

'pluck'
is an obligatory

nostalgia
follows its own beat

call it selective
hearing

tied to little things
doll houses
toy cars
stuffed animals

. . .

it's all a short
jag
down memory land

quelle surprise
your paramour

the sound and the fury
converge

love with one arm
around dread

dread there
ring on the pinky

sun in my eyes

how far in?
fit is not prescriptive

it's alien
not to be blinded

when joy
brings on pain

the point being
(I meant to say)
they're sisters

one's a pushover
the other a basket case

who darkens at
compliments

for family reasons
they walk arm in arm

like praise and glare

don't try to figure
this maligned
happiness

it's bright out!

snow moon

over bare ground

latitude
is a matrix
with older names

defending vanity

non-matched
binaries

still have
a common center

difference
often is adrift

in our sublunary
world

a drab dress
(or a dim bulb)
can hide
reality

example:
the shell and the yoke

Humpty Dumpty
is a hero

without a
designated holiday

bird with a seed

cracks open a tree

blow back
exists on all levels

to continue:

mistletoe grows
golden on the bough
parasitic

as is beauty—
beside the point

. . .

'beside' graphs
onto neutral splendor

vigil
to the pure instant

to tap the phloem

as life raises
to greening leaves

a dangling clause
leaps into place

. . .

breakfast
a quasi-effect
brings the sun
daily each day

if only for
feeling our own

propose

chance events

to let loose
bees in your bonnet

for instance
a perfect four-leaf clover
dead of winter
cupped in ice

rules would have
the aleatory point

elided
right out of existence

turn your future back
from the edge

stop—
just sidestep
the present

confusion
seek your belief

wait

luck
is limpid
as a leprechaun

take provisions
borrow a shillelagha

look around

see the treasure

the wind brought you
atoms of

red Persian gold
turquoise from China
lapis lazuli
dug in the South Seas

breathe deeply

be astonished

tell a friend

a speck of mica

beside a quill

a lapsed correspondence

body
and supposit

isinglass
sees through
the nib
to the provocation

splintered words

that stonewall

the famed image
of logic
as intimacy

the goose
(or gander)
source of words

sees beyond
strictness

the weight of one
feather

on the pans of
justice
and it can balance

the faintest heart

with nothing
to add

dark matter

somehow stole time

(old story, see Homer)

a few billion seconds

then made believe
nothing happened

takes a thief
to catch . . .

wait
remember how you stole

moments
agile and sexy

to be alone with ________

babies are born
spirited away

eras lost
Aion disbanded

your autobiography
cut, rejected
for lack of middle chapters

true

we all seem younger
than we are

wrinkles botoxed

I want to hear
who pocketed the theft

and what it's worth
now

tinny scratch

an ant exes
the laundry list

this moment in
silent disavowal

mice mate in
the kitchen stove

mute unease

like clockwork
meant to trickle
time

into your ear
syncopatedly

off-tempo

it wakes
a heartbeat

somewhere
this time
you don't know whose

pushpin

impolitic meme

'head
for easier removal'

family resemblance
of fasteners

there is the brass version

it does the right thing

look closely
how everything is put together

before God inserted
the tack

there was clatter

there was dissociation

it was the first day

today

take the day off

spread your hands
as if to say, gently now

you know the words
troubled but valiant

whispering
from your lips

as stray drops
from this fact
condense in a cloud
in front of you

you know the feel
of air on your cheeks

some call it love

that diffuse longing
for what you already have

as soul knits with soul

the touch of a
butterfly's wings

the door is open

the sun will chase you
to the hilltop

it's that simple

www.ingramcontent.com/pod-product-compliance
Lightning Source LLC
Chambersburg PA
CBHW022200160726
48282CB00024B/259
9788182539488